The Big Book of
FAITH
QUESTIONS

Gill Hollis and Marcin Piwowarski

CONTENTS

THE BIBLE

Q What is the Bible?

A It is God's Word to us in a collection of sixty-six books.

There are two parts.

The Old Testament contains thirty-nine books including the history of the Jewish nation (and lots of battles), laws, prophecies, songs, proverbs, prayers and words of wisdom. Some of the best stories are here!

The New Testament contains twenty-seven books which record the events of the life, death and resurrection of Jesus, letters to help Christians live as God wants them to, and a vision of the future.

The Bible is the world's bestselling book. Reading it can be a life-changing experience.

Q Who wrote the Bible?

A People inspired by God Himself.

The Bible took about 1,000 years to be written, so it's not clear who wrote it all.

Moses might have written some of the first five books of the Old Testament and many of the Psalms were written by King David. Most of the New Testament letters were written by the apostle Paul; the Gospels were written by Matthew, Mark, Luke and John. All of these people were inspired by God through His Holy Spirit.

The apostle Paul tells his friend Timothy that everything in the Bible is there to help people learn about their faith, correct them when they go wrong, and show them how to live God's way.

Q What's the Bible all about?

A God and His people.

It contains the lives of Abraham, Isaac and Jacob; the account of Joseph being sold as a slave and Moses crossing the Red Sea; the stories of David the shepherd boy killing the giant Goliath and Daniel surviving the den of lions; it contains the story of the first Christmas and the miracles performed by Jesus before He was crucified, died and rose from the dead at Eastertime.

It's the story of how God made the world and about the people God called to follow Him. It's the account of how things went wrong and how God put things right, and His plans for the future.

Q Why is the Bible important?

A It teaches people about God.

If you want to know God then the Bible is the best place to look. The Bible helps people understand what God is like, especially in the stories of Jesus. Jesus showed who God is in a very special way (more about that later). The Bible shows how much Jesus loved God and how He treated other people; anyone who wants to live God's way needs to be like Jesus.

It would be hard to be a Christian without knowing what is in the Bible.

GOD

Q What is God like?

A Holy, fair, loving and forgiving.

Q Who is God?

A Maker of
Heaven and Earth.

The Bible describes God as a loving and caring Creator who created all things 'good' and 'very good'.

Not only did God create planet Earth, but He created stars and planets and the whole of the universe. Nothing exists that He doesn't know about.

God made people, male and female, to be His friends. God knew about each one before they were born and knows people better than they know themselves.

God is all-powerful, all-knowing and holy, beyond all human understanding.

God is good and just, concerned about truth, and completely fair.

God is love. God is like a perfect father: He takes care of His children, providing for their needs, comforting them and giving them what is best for them. God is slow to get angry and quick to show love and forgiveness.

Q How can we know God?
A By learning about Jesus.

God sent Jesus, His Son, to be born as a human being and live among us. His life tells us a lot about God.

Jesus showed us that everyone needs God's forgiveness and that God loves us even when we do not love Him. Jesus told a story about a father whose son came to say sorry to him. The father was just waiting to forgive him. God waits patiently for us to come to Him in the same way.

We can also know God by reading about Him in the Bible and by talking to Him in prayer.

Q Where is God?
A Everywhere!

God is spirit and has no body like ours to keep Him in one place.

God has always existed. God had no beginning, and He has no end. He will never die or disappear. God is there in the deepest ocean, at the top of the highest mountain or in the farthest corner of space. Nothing and no one is hidden from God.

CREATION

Q Who made the world?
A God did.

The Bible starts by describing God's amazing act of creation. It doesn't tell us how He did it but it tells us who made the world and why.

The Bible tells us that God is the Creator of all things and that people are especially important to Him. It also tells us that our human nature shows us something about what God is like.

Q What sort of world did God make?
A A very good world.

As God made mountains and rivers, plants and trees, stars and planets, fish, birds and animals, He saw that they were good. He was pleased with the beautiful world He had created.

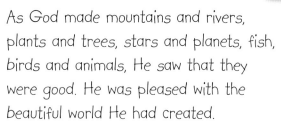

When God made man and woman, He made creatures who could know Him, who could love and be loved, who could think and imagine and create things. Then God saw that it was very good.

Q Why did God make people?

A To be His friends.

People are especially important to God because they are more like Him than any other creature He made.

When God made people they spent time together with Him every day, enjoying each other's company, talking together. God also gave them a job to do, so they could share in His work, caring for His world and the creatures He had made. God told them to have children and to work on the land to grow plants to feed themselves.

Q When did the world go wrong?

A When people disobeyed God.

God wanted the people He had made to love His world and take care of it. God gave them the gift of life and everything they needed to enjoy it and know Him as their friend. He gave them one simple rule. But they decided to ignore the rule and do what they wanted instead.

God was saddened by what they had done. He could not trust them any more. Their friendship was broken.

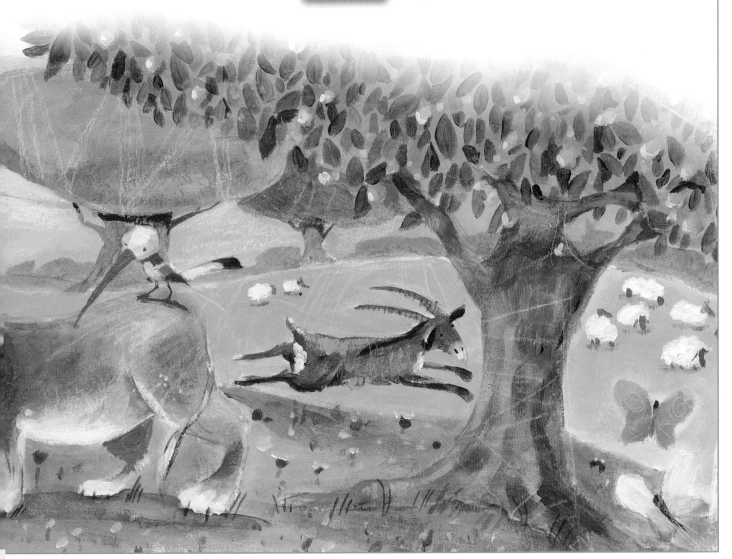

SIN

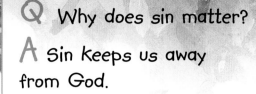

Q What is sin?

A Anything less than perfection.

People sin when they disobey God's rules, but they also sin by thinking or acting in a way which is selfish, unkind or thoughtless. When Adam and Eve disobeyed God, sin became part of what it is to be human – people put themselves before what God wants.

God wants us to love Him and to show it by caring about the people around us, to be kind and generous and to help people in need. He wants us to stand up for people who cannot speak for themselves, and to be a friend to people who have no friends.

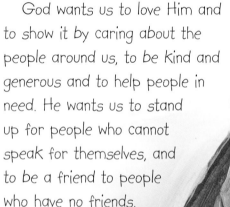

Q Why does sin matter?

A Sin keeps us away from God.

Sin spoilt God's perfect world and all the relationships in it.

God hates it when people tell lies or break important rules because one sin often leads to another. God knows that when people think too much about themselves, they stop caring about others. Being selfish often makes people jealous and cruel. God cannot bear to see people do terrible things to each other.

Q Does God stop loving people who sin?

A No, but ...

God made people to be His friends. When Adam and Eve broke His rules, He could not pretend it hadn't happened. When Cain murdered his brother Abel, God could not say, 'That's OK!' God is not only loving, He is just and fair and good.

The sin, the bad things that happened then and still happen now, had to be punished. God was angry and banished Adam and Eve from the Garden of Eden, but He still looked after them. Cain was sent away but God stopped people from killing him.

Q Is anyone perfect?

A Only Jesus.

God had a plan to deal with sin so that He could be just and loving at the same time.

From the time of Moses, the priest would confess all the sins of the people over a live goat which would 'carry away' the sins of the people. Another goat would be sacrificed as a sign of the sorrow the people felt because of their sin. This happened once a year.

God's plan was to send Jesus, who died once on the cross carrying away the sins of all the world for ever. Anyone who wants God's forgiveness needs to accept that Jesus has taken the punishment for their sin.

ADAM'S DESCENDANTS

Q Why did God send the Flood?

A God planned to start again.

After Abel was killed by Cain, Adam and Eve had another son called Seth. Seth and his family worshipped God. But as more and more people filled the earth, they became selfish and cruel all over again. God was sorry that He had made people and decided to destroy the earth.

Q Did God save anyone?

A Yes, Noah and his family.

There was one man who loved God. God was pleased with Noah and told him to build an ark so that he and his family and all the animals could be safe from the Flood.

After the Flood, God started again. He gave people another chance to love Him and care about each other and His world. God promised He would never flood the whole world again.

Q Why was the tower of Babel built?

A To prove men were great.

Generations later, everyone had forgotten once more about God. This time they were using the skills they had learned to think only about themselves and how great they were. They built a huge tower. God stopped things before they became even worse. He confused their language so they could not understand each other, and scattered them over the earth.

Q What did God ask Abraham to do?

A To trust Him.

God wanted a person, a group of people, a nation, to love Him and live the way He had always intended people to live. He needed someone who would listen and then trust Him whatever happened.

God knew that it would never be the way it had been before Adam and Eve disobeyed Him, but Abraham listened when God spoke to him. Abraham trusted God even when what God wanted seemed really hard to understand. Abraham had faith in God.

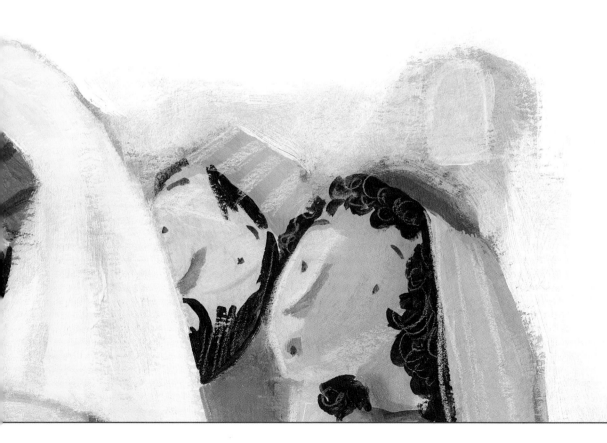

GOD'S PEOPLE

Q What did God promise Abraham?

A Many descendants.

God promised Abraham more descendants than he could count stars in the sky. God told Abraham that He would lead him to a place where he could start a new nation and people.

Abraham was very old and didn't have any children, but he obeyed God and left his home for a new land he knew nothing about. Abraham trusted God even though his wife was very old, and he began to doubt they could have children. God kept His promise and Sarah gave birth to their son Isaac.

Q Who were the Patriarchs?

A Abraham, Isaac and Jacob.

Abraham wanted Isaac to have a wife from his own people, with the same beliefs and customs. So Isaac married Rebekah, granddaughter of Abraham's brother.

Isaac and Rebekah had twin sons, Esau and Jacob. Jacob tricked his brother and his father so that Isaac blessed him rather than Esau, the elder son.

Each family taught their children to trust God. Through these three families God's people grew as He had promised Abraham. At first they were nomads: they lived in tents and moved their families and sheep, goats, camels and donkeys wherever there was fresh water and food.

Q When did God's people become the Israelites?

A After Jacob's death.

Jacob had twelve sons and a daughter, and each son became the head of a large family with many descendants. God renamed Jacob and called him Israel. God's people were then known as the children of Israel or the Israelites by the nations around them.

At the time of Jacob's death, the Israelites were living in Egypt and the Egyptians had made them slaves.

Q Where was the promised land?

A The land of Canaan.

Canaan was a fertile land, described in the Bible as a land flowing with milk and honey. It occupied the land along the coast of the eastern Mediterranean Sea as far as the River Jordan, south of Lebanon and north of Egypt.

God called Moses to lead His people out of Egypt and into the land He had promised them. The King of Egypt didn't want to let them go, but after God had sent many plagues on the Egyptians, the Israelites escaped through the Red Sea, heading for the promised land.

GOD'S RULES

Q How many rules did God give to Moses?

A Ten.

God knew that His people needed a clear set of rules to help them obey Him and care for each other. He called Moses up on to Mount Sinai and gave him ten rules, or commandments. God promised to lead them and always care for them if they followed these rules.

Q When did God give the rules?

A When the Israelites were in the desert.

God had set His people free from slavery in Egypt. Now He needed to set them apart from all the other nations around. Then people would see that God's people were different, a holy people who were like the God they trusted and followed.

God wrote the ten commandments on two large stones.

Q What do the rules say about God?

A That He is holy and special.

The first commandment is this: 'Do not worship any gods except Me.'

The second commandment is: 'Don't make any idols and worship them.'

In the third, God tells His people: 'Do not use My name as a swearword.'

The fourth commandment is about keeping one day a week special on which to rest and worship God, just as He rested after the work of creation.

Q How should we treat other people?

A With love and respect.

The fifth commandment is about how we should treat our parents: 'Respect your father and your mother.'

Commandments six to ten are about how to behave towards other people.

'Do not kill. Be faithful in marriage. Do not steal. Do not tell lies about others. Do not want anything that *belongs* to *someone else* so much that it spoils your friendship with them.'

GOD'S PROMISES

Q Why did God make promises?

A God loved His people.

From the beginning, God made good things. He made people and gave them the gift of life, the ability to share with Him in creation by having children, the food they needed, a place to live.

The people broke His trust when they disobeyed His only rule. But God never gave up. He made agreements with them and their descendants, promising good things for them for as long as they kept certain rules, rules which meant they could live together in peace.

Q What came from God's promise to Abraham?

A A new nation, God's people.

The whole nation of Israel was descended from Abraham.

God promised one of Abraham's descendants, King David, that a king would come from his family who would rule for ever. God kept His promise and, many generations later, that king was born. His name was Jesus.

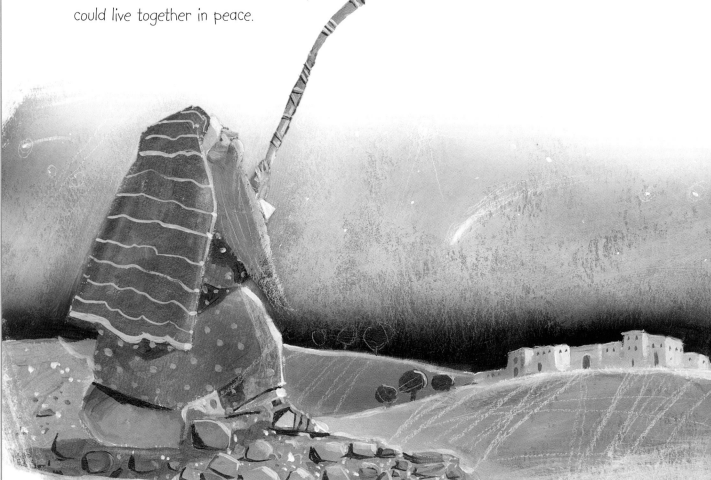

Q What happened when the people broke the agreement?

A They were punished.

God promised to free His people from slavery in Egypt but when He did they complained they were hungry. God provided them with food and water but they soon complained it was boring and they would rather be slaves again in Egypt.

Even when God was giving Moses the ten commandments, the people were so impatient they made a calf out of gold to worship instead of God!

As a punishment, the Israelites wandered through the desert for forty years instead of living in their home in Canaan.

Q Why did God send prophets?

A To give the people another chance.

God kept His promises but His people continually did not keep their side of the agreement. They would not trust Him.

God sent prophets, men and women inspired by Him, to speak to the people, to encourage them and often to warn them to change their ways. But generation after generation ignored the warnings of the prophets. The Israelites were defeated by their enemies and eventually exiled, sent away from their homes and ruled over by other countries.

THE PROPHETS

Q Who made people prophets?

A God.

No one ever volunteered to be a prophet. God chose the people He knew would take His words to His people in their time – and many of them thought of reasons why someone else should do it.

Moses asked God to use his brother Aaron instead. Elijah suffered from depression. Isaiah said he was unworthy.

Jeremiah said he was too young. Jonah ran away because he didn't want to take God's message!

Q What did a prophet do?

A Brought God's messages to the people.

The prophets were called to warn the people about what would happen

The word of God just came to prophets such as Elijah. God spoke to some, such as Isaiah and Ezekiel, in dreams or visions; Micah speaks of being inspired by the Holy Spirit.

What they all had in common was that they trusted God when others could not hear Him. God used them to give the people another chance to repent, to say sorry, ask His forgiveness and change.

Q Why was their job difficult?

A Almost no one listened!

Most of the prophets, such as Jeremiah, were persecuted or made fun of. Some, such as Elijah, were in danger of losing their lives. Nearly all of them were ignored by most people until it was too late.

Jonah ran away, however, not because he was afraid of the Assyrians but because he knew that they might repent when they heard the message! Jonah felt they deserved the punishment of death; he could not understand that God loved His people so much that He wanted to forgive and not destroy them.

Q What messages did they bring?

A Say sorry, change your ways and trust God.

Elijah warned King Ahab to stop worshipping idols made of stone and to turn and trust God alone. Isaiah and Jeremiah warned the people that God would not protect them from other nations if they continued to be cruel and unjust and worship other gods. Amos warned them that God did not want more religious feasts, songs and sacrifices, he wanted them to be kind and fair in all they did. Micah warned of judgment but looked forward to the promise of the One who would save them.

JESUS

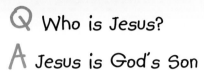

Q Who is Jesus?

A Jesus is God's Son

Jesus has always existed. He was with God when He created the world and He gave life to all the things God made.

Jesus is also called Christ. This is not His surname but means 'the anointed one' in Greek. He is also called the 'Messiah', which has the same meaning in Hebrew. When Jesus was born, God became a man and took human form. He was the one chosen by God to save people from their sins and show them how to be God's friends.

Q When did Jesus live?

A About 2,000 years ago.

Jesus was born when Herod was King of Judea, Caesar Augustus was in charge of the Roman Empire and Quirinius was governor of Syria.

He was born in a tiny part of the Roman Empire called Palestine, into an ordinary working family. Joseph (read about him on page 26) was a carpenter in Nazareth, so Jesus grew up there.

Q What was Jesus like?

A Loving, caring, brave and good.

Jesus was born in the Middle East so it is likely that He had very dark hair and skin, brown eyes and a beard.

The Gospels tell us that Jesus made friends with tax collectors such as Matthew and Zacchaeus whom others hated, and with lepers whom others avoided. He cared about people's needs and on many occasions made sure that hungry people had food.

Jesus was tempted to do wrong, just as we are, but He did not sin. Jesus chose to die a painful death to save others when He could have run away.

Q What did Jesus teach?

A About God and how to love Him.

Jesus taught people to love God first and to love other people as much as they love themselves.

Jesus said that if we want to be forgiven by God, we have to forgive those who have done bad things to us. He said that we should be committed to helping the poor.

Almost everyone thought Jesus was an amazing teacher. He often used stories, or parables, to help them understand what they had never understood before.

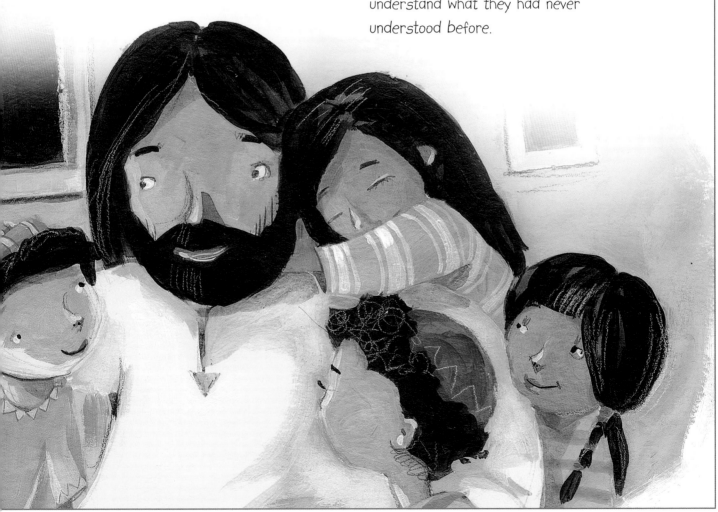

JESUS' BIRTH

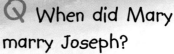

Q When did Mary marry Joseph?

A When she was pregnant.

Q Who was Jesus' mother?

A Mary.

The angel Gabriel told Mary she would have a child who would be called the Son of God. She would become pregnant by the power of the Holy Spirit. It was a miracle.

Mary was still very young, and must have been very frightened, but she loved God and was willing to be the mother of Jesus.

Joseph was preparing to marry Mary before the angel came. When Mary told him what the angel had said, he was sad. Joseph loved Mary but thought he would not be able to marry her if she was going to have a baby that wasn't his.

Another angel came to Joseph to tell him that Mary was carrying God's Son and that he should marry her and be a father to the new baby. So Joseph married Mary and looked after her.

Q Where was Jesus born?

A In a stable in Bethlehem.

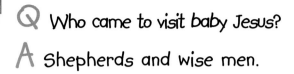

Mary and Joseph lived in Nazareth but had to travel to Bethlehem to be listed in the record books. The Romans, who were in charge of the country, wanted to count all the people in a census.

The town was so busy that there was no room to stay anywhere. As Mary was about to give birth, an innkeeper let them use his stable. When Jesus was born Mary made a bed for Him in a manger, an animals' feeding trough.

Q Who came to visit baby Jesus?

A Shepherds and wise men.

On the night Jesus was born, a choir of angels told some shepherds that their Saviour had been born. They rushed to Bethlehem to look for the newborn baby.

Some time later, wise men, who had followed the movements of an unusual star, came looking for a new king. They brought Jesus gifts: gold fit for a king; frankincense, which was used in worship; and myrrh, which was used in burial.

LIVING GOD'S WAY

Q What did Jesus teach about living a good life?

A 'Be perfect, as God is perfect.'

Q What did Jesus teach about anger?

A It can lead to worse things.

Jesus taught people that God wants great things of them.

Jesus said we are the salt of the world. We need to follow God's ways closely so that other people can see that we are different. Salt that has lost its flavour is no longer good for anything.

Jesus said we are the light of the world. We need not hide away and be ashamed of our faith, but need to make sure people know we love God. Then others might also follow God's ways.

The law of Moses had said that murder was wrong and would be punished. Jesus said that it isn't just the act of murder that is wrong but also the anger or hatred that leads to murder. God wants people to live in peace and to make up any quarrels quickly.

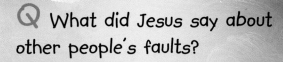

Q What did Jesus teach about forgiveness?

A Don't hold grudges.

Jesus told Peter that God's people should learn to forgive other people as many times as they come to say sorry – just as they themselves want God's forgiveness again and again.

Jesus then told a story about a man who owed a King a huge debt. The King let him off paying the debt – but then heard that the man refused to let off another man who owed him only a small amount. The King was very angry. People who have been forgiven need, in turn, to forgive others.

Q What did Jesus say about other people's faults?

A Don't judge each other.

People should confess their own sins and ask God's help to put them right rather than worrying about the sins of others. Otherwise, Jesus said, it's like looking for a speck of dust in someone's eye when you've got a plank of wood in yours! Only God is in a position to judge.

Jesus told people to love and serve each other, always putting others before themselves. If everyone did this, there would be no fault to find with others, no one to be angry with, no one who needed forgiveness!

MIRACLES

Q Why did Jesus perform miracles?

A To show God's love.

Jesus called His miracles 'signs' because they showed what God was like.

When Jesus calmed a storm on a lake He demonstrated that God has power to control nature and also that He didn't want His friends to be afraid.

When people were healed or Jesus changed five loaves and two little fish to feed 5,000 hungry people, it showed how much God cared about them.

When Jesus raised Lazarus from death, it showed that God had power over death.

Q How did Jesus help people through miracles?

A He showed them God's love and healed people who were ill.

Jesus gave the blind their sight, made the deaf hear, cured people of their skin diseases and healed a man with a withered arm. He healed a soldier's servant without visiting his house and healed a woman who touched the hem of His coat.

Jesus even raised people from the dead: among them Jairus' twelve-year-old daughter, the son of the widow of Nain and Lazarus, brother of Mary and Martha.

Q How did people react?

A With joy, amazement, fear and jealousy.

When Jesus turned water into wine at a wedding, His mother was pleased. She knew He had God's power to make incredible things happen.

When Jesus healed a man who couldn't walk, the people were amazed at His power. But the church leaders were jealous because Jesus also told the man his sins were forgiven - something only God could do. Jesus made enemies as well as friends.

When Jesus walked on water, His disciples were both amazed and afraid, because they saw that He had God's power to control even the laws of nature.

Q Why did the religious leaders hate Jesus?

A Jesus took away some of their power.

Part of Jesus' purpose in being on earth was to use God's power to help people and show that God wanted to forgive anyone who was sorry for their sins.

The religious leaders of the time had been powerful till then. When Jesus healed a man with a withered hand on the Sabbath day, it did not break one of God's rules, but one of theirs. Jesus said it was right to do good things on the Sabbath. The religious leaders were so angry that they started to plot His death.

LOVE

Q Who should we love?

A God and our neighbour.

Jesus reminded people that they should love God with all their heart and soul and strength and love their neighbour as much as they love themselves. If people put all their energy into doing this, they would be keeping all the commandments that God gave to Moses.

This kind of love is not about how we feel, but about how we behave. It's caring for others and putting them first, even when we don't feel like it.

Q Who are our neighbours?

A Anyone who needs our help.

Jesus told the story of the Good Samaritan to answer this question.

When a Jewish man was beaten up by robbers and left lying dying in the road, two religious people walked by without helping him; but a Samaritan – a foreigner and an enemy of the Jews – stopped, took him to an inn to be cared for and paid for his treatment. Jesus said everyone should show love for people as this Samaritan did.

Q What did Jesus say about our enemies?

A He told us to love them too.

Jesus told His disciples to pray for anyone who treated them badly. He said that if someone hit them on one cheek, they should turn the other to be hit too. If someone asked them to walk with them one mile, they should offer to walk two miles.

Anyone who loves God should repay evil with good, for only then will they show God's love; only then will they be different from everyone around them and show that God's way is the best way.

Q How can we love God?

A By obeying Him and loving other people.

Jesus told a story about what would happen at the end of time. God would welcome those who had given Him food when He was hungry or drink when He was thirsty; He would be pleased with those who had given Him clothes and somewhere to stay when He had nothing, or had looked after Him when He was ill, and visited Him in prison.

When those people asked Him when they had ever done these things for Him, they were told this: that if they had ever done anything kind for someone in need, they had done it for Him.

JESUS' CRUCIFIXION

Q What was crucifixion?

A A punishment for criminals.

The Romans used crucifixion as a form of execution.

Criminals were whipped and, when they were weak, nailed by the wrists and ankles to a wooden cross and left hanging by the side of the road until they died, thirsty and in terrible pain. This could take many hours.

Q Where was Jesus crucified?

A At Golgotha, outside the city walls.

During His trial the night before, Jesus had had no sleep. He had been beaten and mocked and was already weak when He carried His cross, stumbling, to the place where people were crucified. This was alongside the main public road outside Jerusalem, at a rocky place that looked like a skull. Jesus was crucified between two thieves.

Q Who wanted Jesus crucified?

A The religious leaders.

The leaders of the Pharisees, the strict Jewish group, hated Jesus. They had many more rules than God had given His people. When Jesus tried to tell the people how much God loved them, and that they needed only to obey God's ten rules, they were angry. They could not believe Jesus had God's power and came from God.

Q How long was Jesus on the cross?

A Six hours.

Jesus was nailed to the cross at 9 o'clock in the morning, and was dead by 3 o'clock in the afternoon.

Jesus asked God to forgive the men who nailed Him to the cross. When one of the thieves put his faith in Him while he hung there, Jesus told the man he would be in Paradise with Him that day. Jesus also asked John to look after His mother before crying out, 'It is finished.' Then Jesus died.

JESUS' DEATH AND BURIAL

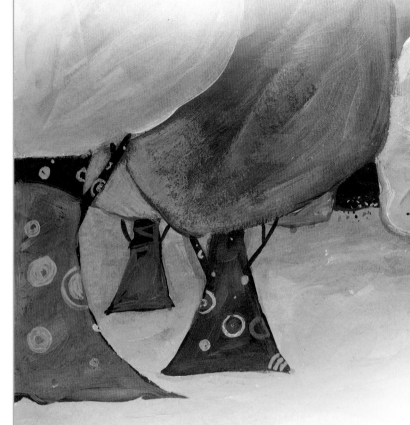

Q What happened after Jesus died?

A He was buried in someone else's tomb.

Q Did Jesus really die?

A Yes.

It was Friday and the religious leaders did not want anyone on the crosses on the Sabbath day. They asked Pilate, the Roman governor, if they could break the legs of the men to make them die more quickly. Then the bodies could be taken down.

The soldiers broke the legs of the two thieves but when they came to Jesus, they saw that He was already dead. Instead, a soldier plunged a sword into His side and blood and water poured out.

After Jesus had died, Joseph of Arimathea, a rich disciple, asked Pilate if he could have His body to bury it. He wrapped it in a clean linen cloth. Then Joseph put Jesus' body in a tomb cut into the side of a rock. A huge, heavy stone was rolled across the entrance. The Pharisees remembered that Jesus had said He would rise from death, so they asked Pilate to put guards outside the tomb, to prevent anyone stealing the body and claiming He had risen.

Q What did Jesus' death achieve?

A Forgiveness for all who trust Him.

The events of Good Friday when Jesus died on the cross were horrible. Jesus did not deserve to die a cruel death. But His death was part of the plan that God had at the beginning to deal with the problem of punishing sin.

God sent Jesus to be the Saviour of the world. When Jesus died, He took the punishment that each person who ever sinned should have. Jesus rescued the world from death. His death meant all who trusted Him could be forgiven.

Q How can I be forgiven?

A Believe that Jesus died in your place.

Anyone who knows that they have done things wrong, and accepts that Jesus died on the cross taking away their sin, will be forgiven. The apostle Paul and his friend Silas told their jailer in Philippi that he could be saved by believing and being baptised.

Paul told the church in Rome that everyone sins and needs to be forgiven by God. God now offers the free gift of forgiveness and life in heaven after death to anyone who believes in Him.

JESUS' RESURRECTION

Q What did the women find out on the first Easter Day?

A Jesus was no longer dead.

Very early on the Sunday morning, the third day after Jesus' death, some women went to the tomb to anoint His body with herbs and spices. They saw that the huge stone had been rolled away from the entrance and that Jesus' body had gone. Two angels appeared and told them, 'Jesus isn't here. He has been raised from death!' The women ran to tell the disciples the amazing news.

Q Who was the first to see Jesus alive?

A Mary Magdalene.

Mary Magdalene stayed by the tomb, very upset because at first she could not understand what had happened. Then she met a man in the garden whom she thought was the gardener. When He spoke her name, she knew at once that it was Jesus, risen from the dead and very much alive!

Q Was Jesus a ghost?

A No, but He had a new kind of body.

After Easter Day Jesus was able to appear in the room where His friends were staying although the door was locked. Jesus also disappeared suddenly without using a door or window.

But Jesus wasn't a ghost. He showed the disciples the nail marks in His hands. He invited Thomas to touch Him. Jesus ate bread and fish with the disciples and He prepared a meal for them on the beach after they'd been fishing one night.

Q Did Jesus stay on earth?

A No, He went back to heaven.

Jesus was seen by Mary Magdalene, eleven of His twelve disciples, two friends walking to Emmaus and by more than 500 believers. He talked and ate with them for forty days.

Finally He met His friends on a mountain in Galilee. He told them to stay in Jerusalem and wait for the Holy Spirit to come and give them power so that they could tell everyone about Him. Then a cloud covered Jesus and took Him upwards.

When the cloud disappeared, two men in white stood there and said, 'Jesus has been taken into heaven.'

THE HOLY SPIRIT

Q Who is the Holy Spirit?

A The presence of God on earth.

God the Father, God the Son and God the Holy Spirit are all one God. The Trinity is the name for all three together.

So the Holy Spirit is God. He has always existed. He was there when the world was created, moving over the things that were made. Just like the wind, which can be felt even when you cannot see it, the Holy Spirit is there and can be known by the effect He has on people and events.

Q What happened at the festival of Pentecost?

A The Holy Spirit came to the believers.

Jesus promised that the Holy Spirit would come to help the believers after He returned to His Father God in heaven. When they gathered in Jerusalem for the feast of Pentecost they heard a sound like a mighty wind and they saw what looked like flames resting on each of them. The Holy Spirit gave them power to speak in many languages and to be brave enough to talk about Jesus to all the foreign visitors who had travelled to Jerusalem for the festival.

Q What does the Holy Spirit do?

A Helps or gives power to God's people.

Jesus described the Holy Spirit as the 'Helper'. The Holy Spirit gives people God's power and wisdom to do God's work. He helps them become more like Jesus. He shows people what God is like, reminding them of God's words and helping them to recognise when they have done something wrong. The Holy Spirit helps people to pray.

Q How does the Holy Spirit help the church?

A He gives many different gifts.

The apostle Paul told the believers in Corinth that the Holy Spirit would give them the power to work miracles, to heal, to preach, to teach, to have faith, to prophesy, to understand what God was saying, to speak and understand different languages and to help people.

Paul said that the Holy Spirit gives different gifts to everyone in the church so that they can help and encourage each other. Every one of them is important.

THE CHURCH

Q What is a church?

A A group of Christian believers.

Although we usually use the word church to mean a building, any gathering of believers is a church, wherever they meet. The first believers, who met in Jerusalem after the Holy Spirit came, are sometimes called the Early Church. Peter was the leader of the first Christians. He described the Church as being built of 'living stones': they were people, not buildings.

Q Who can belong to the church?

A Anyone who trusts Jesus.

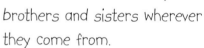

The apostle Paul told the church in Galatia that all believers are equal: men and women, Jewish or any other nationality, slaves or free men and women – all are God's children, and therefore one family of brothers and sisters wherever they come from.

Q What is the church for?

A Encouraging each other.

The Early Church met to worship God, pray, sing hymns, encourage and help each other. They ate together, shared everything they had and gave money to the poor.

The church does the same today, helping Christians to live as God's people during the rest of the week. The church meets in churches or cathedrals, people's homes, community centres or school halls. In some countries, where it is illegal to be a Christian, the church has to meet in secret.

Q Why are there different kinds of church?

A People like to worship God in different ways.

Some people like formal services and times of quiet; others like more freedom. Finding the right church means choosing people who help you to serve God in the best way. It also means finding the place where the gifts God has given you can be used.

Paul describes the church as the Body of Christ. It is made up of lots of parts, not just one: a body is not all ears or all arms – there are eyes and mouth, hands and feet. Each part has work to do, a gift to be used to do something useful for God.

BAPTISM

Q Who baptised
his followers?

A John the Baptist, who was
preparing the way for Jesus.

When people came to John, he told
them that they needed to repent, to
say sorry for their sins and be baptised
in the River Jordan. Then they needed
to change their ways and live as God
wanted.

The people would walk into the river
and be ducked under the water by

John. He was not washing
away dirt; the water was
a sign that their sins were
forgiven.

Q Why was Jesus
baptised?

A He knew it was what
God wanted.

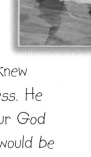

Jesus asked John to baptise
Him in the River Jordan. John knew
that Jesus had no sins to confess. He
knew that Jesus was the Saviour God
had promised. He even said it would be
better if Jesus baptised him!

But John did as Jesus asked. As Jesus
came up out of the water, a
voice from heaven said: 'This
is My Son and I am pleased
with Him.'

Q What happens at a baptism?

A Water is used as a symbol of sin washed away.

Q Who can be baptised now?

A Anyone who wants to follow Jesus.

Jesus told His friends to make disciples throughout the world and to baptise them. On the Day of Pentecost, Peter told people to follow God's ways and be baptised so that their sins would be forgiven. Three thousand people were baptised that day!

Anyone can be baptised if they believe that Jesus died for them and want to live the way He taught His disciples.

Parents can bring their babies to church to be baptised. Water that has been blessed is sprinkled on the child's forehead and the child is welcomed into the Christian family after parents have made promises on their behalf.

Adults or new Christians can make their own promises to follow Jesus. They can be baptised in a baptistry, a pool or a river. They are guided under the water as a symbol of dying to their old life, and come up from the water as a symbol of rising to live a new life with Jesus.

HOLY COMMUNION

Q Why do believers celebrate Holy Communion?

A Jesus told His disciples to do so.

On the night before He died, Jesus ate a final meal with His twelve disciples. He took some bread, broke it and shared it with His friends, saying, 'This is My body, given for you. Take and eat it.' Later in the meal Jesus took a cup of wine. He said, 'This is My blood, shed for you.'
Jesus told His friends to remember Him whenever they ate bread and drank wine together.

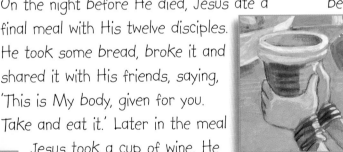

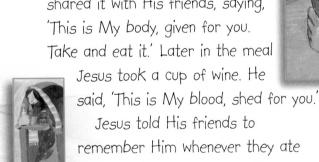

Q What happens at Holy Communion?

A Believers remember Jesus' death.

From the time of the Early Church, believers broke bread and drank wine in a special way to remember Jesus as He had told them to – and the sacrifice that He made when He died on the cross.

Most Christian churches still do this by having a Communion service regularly. It might be called the Lord's Supper, the Eucharist or the Mass, but believers are invited to eat bread or a special wafer and take a sip of wine or juice in memory of Jesus.

Q Who can take part in the service?

A Believers who have openly declared their faith.

The service of Holy Communion is a very special one. When *believers* eat the bread and drink the wine, they are taking part in something special. They are admitting they know they are sinful and need Jesus' forgiveness and strength to live the way God wants them to. They are showing that they want to thank Jesus for dying in their place.

Many churches want *believers* to be baptised or confirmed or to declare their faith in a special service once in their lives before taking part regularly.

Q What else happens in the church service?

A Bible readings, prayers, songs and a talk.

There will usually be one or more readings of Bible passages. There will be prayers for anyone who needs help, and songs or hymns praising God. There will also be a short talk to teach the people there, usually by explaining a Bible passage.

Different churches may include these things at different places in the service.

PRAYER

Q What is prayer?

A A conversation with God.

People should praise God, telling Him how much they love Him. They should say sorry for things they have done wrong, and thank God for all the things He has done for them.

Jesus said that when people pray, they should remember that God is like a father who wants to give good gifts to His children. God knows what we need even before we ask. We should use simple words, listen for an answer and trust God to do what is best.

Q What is the Lord's Prayer?

A A pattern for prayer that Jesus taught His friends.

'Our Father in heaven,
hallowed be Your name,
Your kingdom come,
Your will be done
on earth as it is in heaven.
Give us today our daily bread.
Forgive us for doing wrong,
as we forgive others.
And lead us not into temptation,
but deliver us from the evil one.'

Q When should I pray?
A Any time you want!

You can talk to God at any time. And He wants you to. It's best though also to have a special time at least once a day to talk to Him. You can pray when you're sad, when you're happy, when you want help for you or for other people. You can thank Him, say sorry, and ask Him for what you need. Jesus prayed to God often when He was on earth, so we can and should too.

Q How should I pray?
A By talking and listening to God.

You can pray anywhere (out loud or silently) at any time and whatever you're doing. You can kneel to show that you want to serve God, or you can keep your eyes shut to help you keep your mind on praying ... But you don't have to do either of these things. Just talk to God like you would to your best friend or a loving father. The most important thing is to be honest with Him - don't pretend. Tell Him how you feel. He knows what you're thinking! And remember to listen to Him.

MONEY

Q What is money for?

A To give us what we need to live.

In the Old Testament Jacob promised that if God would give him the food and clothing he needed, then he would give back a tenth of it for God to use.

King David recognised that everything he had came from God, and he was just looking after it, giving it back so God could use it.

Jesus told His disciples that they must not worry about what they should eat or wear, because God would provide them with all they needed.

Q Can rich people be friends of Jesus?

A Yes, but it may be hard.

A rich man came to Jesus and asked Him: 'How can I have eternal life?' Jesus was pleased that the man kept God's commandments, but told him to do one more thing: sell everything and give the money to the poor.

The man was very rich and went away sadly. If the choice was between God and money, he wanted money more. Jesus said it was hard for rich people to enter God's kingdom.

Q How should we give money away?

A Cheerfully.

The apostle Paul said that God loves people who are happy when they give money away to help other people. It is not so much about how much you give, but whether you need what you have left.

Jesus watched a poor woman giving her last coins to the work of the Temple. Jesus said her small amount was worth more because others had given from the large amount they had while she had given everything.

Q Who should receive the money we give away?

A Anyone who needs it.

The apostle Paul told the first Christians that God had given them enough so they could share with anyone else who needed help, and he encouraged them to give generously and to offer hospitality to other people. Paul also said that people who gave much away would receive much; those who gave little would receive little.

Christians today give to many causes, including their own church building and those who work there; local charities; missionaries and other people who work for God; and people in other countries who are in need.

FOLLOWING JESUS

Q How can people follow Jesus today?

A By living the way God wants them to.

Paul sent a letter to the church in Colossae. He said, 'Now you are Christians you must stop being angry, hateful and saying unkind things about others. Instead, be gentle, kind, humble and patient. Forgive anyone who does you wrong. The most important thing is to love each other.'

Q What good things should believers do?

A Be honest, fair and kind to others.

When Zacchaeus, the tax collector, met Jesus, he gave up cheating people and stealing from them. Zacchaeus promised to give people back more than he had taken from them and to share what he had with the poor.

Once people have met Jesus, their lives change. They want to do good things. The disciples in the Early Church shared what they had, were kind to one anther and gave people things they needed. People today can give to many different charities even if they don't know someone in need of help.

Q **What should a Christian be like?**

A **Like Jesus.**

The apostle Paul told the church in Galatia that the Holy Spirit would help Christians be like Jesus. His characteristics are to be loving, happy, peacemaking, patient, kind, good, faithful, gentle and to have self-control.

Christians don't become perfect overnight, but their lives change gradually as a result of knowing Jesus and listening to what God wants of them.

Q **What happens when believers do wrong things?**

A **They tell God and say sorry.**

God promises to forgive people if they are really sorry and confess their sin. To thank God for His forgiveness, it's important to live the way He intended. Paul told the church in Rome that once they had become believers they would be more aware of what sin is and would be tempted to continue to do things that they knew were wrong.

SUFFERING

Q Why is there suffering in the world?

A Because people have choices.

God made Adam and Eve so that they could choose whether to listen to God or not. They chose to go their way instead of God's way. When Adam and Eve sinned, the world stopped being perfect. Theirs was the first suffering, when God sent them away from Eden.

Cain's jealousy caused Abel's death; much suffering since then has been because people choose to do things which hurt other people instead of trying to do good things, as God wants.

Q Why do people die in poverty?

A The rich do not share their wealth.

God made a world rich in many good things. God told us not to be greedy but to share what we have and to care about other people, especially if they need our help. No one can make other people share if they want to keep things for themselves, so poor people suffer and die.

Q Why do natural disasters happen?

A Sometimes because people have not looked after God's world.

Some natural disasters are caused because people have cut down too many trees so there is more flooding in the world; the pollution caused by careless people has destroyed the delicate balance of the way the world works.

Instead of caring for the physical world, people down the ages have taken more than they need without thinking about the consequences for other people, other nations or future generations. This has caused ice caps to melt, the climate to change and bad effects in many parts of the world.

Q Does God care when people suffer?

A Yes, God hates suffering and injustice of every kind.

God's rules have always made provision for the poor, widows and orphans, strangers and homeless people. He was angry with His people when they were unjust, cruel, thoughtless and greedy.

God sent Jesus who had compassion on the sick and sad, and took away their pain and suffering. When His friend Lazarus died, Jesus cried.

Finally, God suffered when Jesus died on the cross. In that death He knew pain, suffering, loneliness and loss.

HEAVEN

Q What is heaven?

A A place where God is.

Jesus taught a prayer which began, 'Our Father, who is in heaven.' God is in heaven.

Jesus said that He came from heaven and was going back there. After His resurrection from the dead, Jesus ascended to heaven.

Jesus described it in picture language as a house with many rooms. He was going there to prepare a place for everyone who loves Him. He promised to be there with His friends.

Q What is heaven like?

A A happy place.

The Bible describes heaven as being a place where there is no more sin, suffering, sadness, pain or death. God will wipe all tears away.

There will be no hatred, unkindness or bullying in heaven; no war or fighting; no jealousy or stealing. Heaven is a place where there is peace and no one has any

reason to be unhappy. Nothing that spoils life on earth will be there.

Q Who will be in heaven?

A Anyone who trusted Jesus.

God will be there with His people and will live with them. Believers who have died will go and live with God and be with Him forever.

When Thomas, one of the disciples, asked Jesus the way to heaven, Jesus replied, 'I am the way, the truth and the life. No one comes to the Father except through Me.' Jesus showed people the way to live and through His death made it possible for anyone to be forgiven their sin and be God's friend.

Q What can you take with you to heaven?

A Nothing but yourself.

Jesus told a story about a man who had spent his life making himself wealthy. He believed that he should make himself comfortable, then eat, drink and be happy. But he died, and could take none of his wealth with him. After his death others enjoyed the things he had spent his life working for.

Jesus said it is more important to work at being kind and generous and helping other people, because these are like treasures in heaven, and nothing can rot or rust them like things on earth.

THE JOURNEY OF FAITH

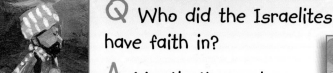

Q What is faith?

A Believing in and trusting God.

God asked Abraham to trust Him. Abraham was very old when God asked him to take a long journey, but he obeyed God, leaving his home for a new land he knew nothing about. There, even though his wife was too old to have children, Sarah gave birth to their son Isaac. Abraham believed and obeyed and God kept His promise.

Sometimes Abraham doubted God and went back to ask Him again whether he had understood correctly what God had promised. But Abraham did have faith.

Q Who did the Israelites have faith in?

A Mostly themselves.

God asked the Israelites, the Jewish nation, to trust Him as Abraham trusted Him. God gave them manna to eat, water to drink and all they needed, including a land to live in.

When things were good, they trusted God. As soon as it became difficult, they looked for someone else to believe in. Usually they believed in the idols the nations around them worshipped. Sometimes they believed in themselves and decided they didn't need God any more. Their journey of faith took them through the wilderness and into the promised land, then into exile and back again.

Q Why did the wise men follow the star?

A To find the promised King.

The wise men were scientists, not Jewish believers. They studied prophecies and the stars and believed a new King had been born. They took a risk by making a long journey from the East until they found Jesus. When they reached Bethlehem, they knew they had found the one they were looking for. Then they responded with what they had. They offered Him their gifts and worshipped Him.

Q Why did Thomas have faith?

A He saw Jesus for himself.

After the resurrection all the disciples saw Jesus except Thomas. He would not believe until he saw Jesus alive for himself. He believed when Jesus came to him. Jesus said, 'Happy are those people who have not seen and yet believe.'

Anyone who has put their faith in God is one of those happy people. They have not seen for themselves but they have trusted the accounts of eyewitnesses. Faith begins when people learn about God and decide that they are sure He can be trusted. It is the beginning of a journey.

WHY AM I HERE?

Q Does God know who I am?

A Yes, He made you and loves you.

God made all people and knows them. King David wrote a song in which he said that God knew him even when he was in his mother's womb and had already planned what good things David could do one day.

Each person is therefore special. God waits for people to come to know Him and, as Jesus told people in the story of the lost sheep, God the shepherd is not happy until every last person is safe and where they should be.

Q How can I know God loves me?

A He gave Jesus to die on a cross.

God's plan from the beginning was that the people He made should know Him and love Him. When they sinned, God set about redeeming them, buying them back again, making everything right.

When Jesus died on the cross, God redeemed the people He had made because He loved them. Jesus died once, and that was enough. God invites everyone to be forgiven, to start again and to be His friend.

Q What can I give to God?

A Yourself - everything you are and everything you have.

And everyone has something that God can use. He gave everyone gifts. God can use whatever anyone gives Him and do great things with it.

When Jesus wanted to find food for more than 5,000 hungry people, a boy offered his lunch of five small rolls and two little fish. Jesus took that food and, by a miracle, fed all the people there – and there were leftovers!

Q What is the purpose of life?

A To love God and keep His commandments.

God gave King Solomon great wisdom and understanding. God also gave him wealth and power. When he was an old man, he looked back on his life and realised that the duty of all the people who have ever lived is simply to love and respect God and keep His rules. Nothing else matters. Everything else seems pointless; it has no lasting value.

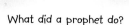
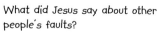

Index of Bible Stories: